Elephant

DK Watch me grow

LONDON, NEW YORK, MUNICH,
MELBOURNE and DELHI

Written and edited by Lisa Magloff
Designed by Sonia Moore and
Mary Sandberg

Publishing Manager Sue Leonard
Managing Art Editor Clare Shedden
Jacket Design Tony Chung
Picture Researcher Liz Moore
Production Shivani Pandey
DTP Designer Almudena Díaz

First published in Great Britain in 2005 by
Dorling Kindersley Limited
80 Strand, London WC2R 0RL

A Penguin Company

ISBN 1-4053-0844-3

Colour reproduction by Media, Development and Printing Ltd.
Printed and bound by South China Printing Co, Ltd., China

see our complete catalogue at

www.dk.com

Contents

Come walk with us and watch us grow!

I'm an elephant

I am very big. I live with a lot of other elephants in a herd. I use my long trunk to put food and water into my mouth.

Elephant skin is very rough and bumpy.

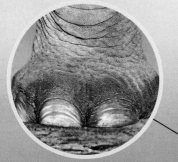

An elephant's foot has thick padding.

Elephants can flap their ears like giant fans, to help them cool off.

Now follow me...turn the page and watch me grow.

Elephants can have long tusks.

The elephant can use its trunk to smell and to pick things up.

Mum and Dad

My Mum lives in a herd with other mothers, babies, and young elephants. Dad likes to live on his own. Mum and Dad met at the water hole.

This is my Mum...

Living in a herd
The leader of the herd is the oldest female elephant. She leads the herd to where water and food can be found.

and this is my Dad – look at his BIG ears!

Male elephants live alone or with small groups of other males.

7

I'm one hour old

I grew inside my mother for nearly two years. After I'm born, other elephants stand nearby to protect me until I'm strong enough to walk.

I'm very weak and wobbly.

Just born
Newborn elephants are very messy, so Mum has to clean her baby off before he can stand up.

Mum gently helps her
baby to his feet.

Messy bath

My favourite time of day is when we all go for a mud bath. The mud is slippery, but it keeps the bugs away. Mum makes sure I am all covered in mud.

Mud protects against sunburn, and keeps elephants cool and free from insect pests.

The tiny calf slides around in the mud, but Mum stays nearby to lend a steady trunk.

Up we go...

Mum pushes her calf up the steep bank. It will be many weeks before he is strong enough to do this by himself.

I'm three months old

I like to play and wrestle with other young elephants. My trunk keeps flopping around, and I can't wait until I am strong enough to use it.

Elephant facts

Adult elephants sleep standing up. Baby elephants sometimes lie down to sleep.

Every day, an adult elephant can make a pile of poo that weighs more than you!

The baby will drink his mother's milk for about five years.

Danger!

Adult elephants are too big to have many enemies, but baby elephants are in danger of attack.

crocodile

cheetah

Crossing the river

When I'm six months old, the rains come and the rivers fill up. We have to cross to get to the better grass on the other side. I stay close to Mum while we cross.

In deep water, adult elephants help the babies by lifting and pushing them through the water.

The trunk makes a handy snorkel.

Underwater fun

Elephants may be big, but this does not stop them from being strong swimmers. They enjoy swimming and will even swim in the ocean.

Learning to feed myself

I still drink milk from my Mum, but now I can pick up food with my trunk too. My family spends hours eating every day.
We eat grass, plants, seeds, and fruit.

The young elephants eat food that's found close to the ground.

The tall adults pluck leaves from the trees.

Twist and pull

Elephants use their trunks to pluck leaves and to pull up tasty plants. This elephant is going to chew the bark off this branch.

17

I'm five years old

Now I have a baby sister. I will help teach her all about how to be an elephant, just like the other elephants taught me. It will be ten more years before I am all grown up.

This is me.

Growing up
Elephants grow very slowly and can live to be 60 or even 80 years old. Male elephants leave the herd when they are around 13.

My baby sister and I walk with Mum.

19

The circle of life goes round and round

Now you know how I turned into a grown-up elephant.

My friends from around the world

There are three types of elephant: Asian, African, and Indian.

Asian elephants are often used to lift heavy logs in the jungle.

Asian elephants have small ears and bumpy heads.

The African elephant has long tusks and very big ears.

Come for a ride!

I'm a baby African Elephant.

This Indian elephant has been decorated for a festival.

Elephant facts

Elephants spend about 16 hours a day eating, and only 3 to 5 hours sleeping.

Elephants cool off using their ears. Blood moves around their ears and cools off as it goes.

The elephant is related to the dugong, a kind of sea cow that lives in shallow waters.

Glossary

Bull
Another name for a male elephant who is fully grown.

Herd
A group of elephants who live and travel together.

Cow
A female who is fully grown and can have babies.

Hide
An elephant's skin, which is very rough and bumpy.

Calf
A very young elephant who is less than five years old.

Tusks
Long, sharp teeth used for digging and gathering food.

Acknowledgments

The publisher would like to thank the following for their kind permission to reproduce their photographs:
(Key: a=above; c=centre; b=below; l=left; r=right; t=top)
1 DigitalVision: Gerry Ellis c. 2-3 Still Pictures: Dianne Blell.
4 DigitalVision: Gerry Ellis cfl. 4-5 DigitalVision: Gerry Ellis.
5 OSF/photolibrary.com: Gerry Ellis/Digital Vision fr. 5 Zefa Visual Media: Steve Craft/Masterfile bcl. 6-7 Getty Images: Taxi/Stan Osolinski. 7 Andy Rouse Wildlife Photography: c.
8 OSF/photolibrary.com: Martyn Colbeck cl. 8-9 OSF/photolibrary.com: Martyn Colbeck. 10-11 OSF/photolibrary.com: Peter Lillie.
11 ImageState/Pictor: bcr. 11 Science Photo Library: Tony Camacho tr.
12-13 DigitalVision: Gerry Ellis. 13 DK Images: Irv Beckman crb; Jerry Young cr. 14 FLPA: Frans Lanting/Minden Pictures car. 14-15 N.H.P.A.: Martin Harvey. 15 Getty Images: Cousteau Society/The Image Bank tcl.

16 Corbis: Jeff Vanuga bl. 16 DigitalVision: Gerry Ellis c. 16-17 FLPA: David Hosking. 17 N.H.P.A.: Ann & Steve Toon car. 18 Bruce Coleman Ltd: cl. 18-19 Alamy Images: Steve Bloom. 20 Alamy Images: Martin Harvey cl. 20 Corbis: Martin Harvey/Gallo Images cb. 20 DigitalVision: Gerry Ellis c. 20 DK Images: Shaen Adey cbl. 20 ImageState/Pictor: Nigel Dennis bcr. 20 OSF/photolibrary.com: IFA-Bilderteam Gmbh cra; Martyn Colbeck ca, car. 20 Andy Rouse Wildlife Photography: tl. 20 Safari Bill Wildlife Photography: crb. 21 DigitalVision: c. 22 Ardea.com: Tom & Pat Leeson bl. 22 DK Images: Dave King c. 22 DigitalVision: Gerry Ellis tl.
22-23 Corbis: Paul Almasy. 23 DigitalVision: Gerry Ellis tr, br.
23 OSF/photolibrary.com: Peter Lillie cr. 24 DigitalVision: car; Gerry Ellis cla, cr, cbr. 24 FLPA: cl. 24 OSF/photolibrary.com: Martyn Colbeck cbl.
All other images © Dorling Kindersley
For further information see: www.dkimages.com